T0157571

"Wow!" was my first reaction when I read this book. This is a powerful and valuable resource that allows and acknowledges grief, fear, anger, and sadness and offers simple strategies to help move through these phases on the way to recovery and wellness. I will highly recommend this gem to all my patients.

—Dr. Karen White, medical oncologist

Person-centred care has become a primary goal in modern medicine. A vital first step is listening to the voice of our patients. A second is to provide tools that aid resilience. This book offers both. Written in a clear voice from a person who has recovered from cancer and has an extensive history in positive psychology, it provides history, lessons from different cultures, and simple advice. It is written for cancer but could offer support in any health environment where people find themselves vulnerable in the face of serious illness.

—Associate Professor, Neil Orford, intensive care specialist

Profoundly emotional and life-changing, cancer has marked too many lives. It need not define us. A positive attitude on cancer's darkest days can make it a transformative experience.

Sue Mackey's book touches my heart. It's a wise and uplifting collection of gems to nurture, empower, and help heal your mental and spiritual insides—during diagnosis and treatment and beyond—into a renewed sense of hope, growth, and wholeness.

Keep it close by you, listen to it, and dip into its comfort. Let it guide you towards sustained health and a new purposeful phase of your life.

—Nerida Kinross-Smith, psychologist

POSITIVE ONCOLOGY

AN OPTIMISTIC APPROACH TO THE BIG C

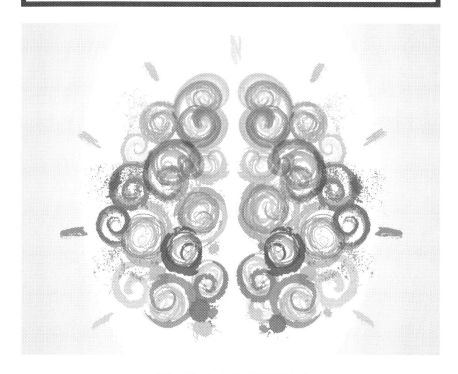

SUE MACKEY

BALBOA.
PRESS

A DIVISION OF HAY HOUSE

Balboa Press books may be ordered through booksellers or by contacting:

Balboa Press
A Division of Hay House
1663 Liberty Drive
Bloomington, IN 47403
www.balboapress.com.au
1 (877) 407-4847

Because of the dynamic nature of the Internet, any web addresses or links contained in this book may have changed since publication and may no longer be valid. The views expressed in this work are solely those of the author and do not necessarily reflect the views of the publisher, and the publisher hereby disclaims any responsibility for them.

The author of this book does not dispense medical advice or prescribe the use of any technique as a form of treatment for physical, emotional, or medical problems without the advice of a physician, either directly or indirectly. The intent of the author is only to offer information of a general nature to help you in your quest for emotional and spiritual well-being. In the event you use any of the information in this book for yourself, which is your constitutional right, the author and the publisher assume no responsibility for your actions.

Any people depicted in stock imagery provided by Thinkstock are models, and such images are being used for illustrative purposes only.
Certain stock imagery © Thinkstock.

Print information available on the last page.

ISBN: 978-1-5043-0663-8 (sc)
ISBN: 978-1-5043-0674-4 (e)

Balboa Press rev. date: 02/20/2017

For Chris, Rowan, Joanna and Ellie.

CONTENTS

INTRODUCTION

This book uses positive psychology principles and provides simple, optimistic strategies to help manage beyond a cancer diagnosis. By paying more attention to choice, perspective, and language, you can practice strengthening your mind to improve your positivity and resilience.

Positive psychology can help reduce your stress levels and supercharge your immune system's response to cancer. Modern science has shown us that the mind controls the brain and the brain can influence the body even at the level of our individual cells. The aim of this approach is to assist you to improve your well-being and healing capacity by using your very own master controller: your mind. Current medical treatments for cancer focus predominantly on drugs, surgery, and radiotherapy to heal the body. With the medical need to focus on saving lives, the ancient wisdom of the connections between mind and body have been over shadowed. Mind and body are inextricably linked. There is a strong correlation between mind strength and body strength.

There are increasing numbers of people surviving cancer and living longer with cancer. There has been a lack of emphasis on psychological support during and after treatment. Having cancer predisposes you and your loved ones to greater challenges with your mental health. For those people going through cancer, this book is recommended as an adjunct to conventional treatments. It offers strategies to develop a more favourable mindset and greater resilience. I like to call this approach *positive oncology*.

ACKNOWLEDGE YOUR GRIEF

Life is difficult. This is a great truth, one of the greatest truths.

—M. Scott Peck, *The Road Less Travelled*

A day you will never forget is the day you are diagnosed with cancer. It happened to me, and my first reaction was to cry for days.

Life consists of ups and downs. Cancer is one of the biggest shocks we can be challenged by. Being faced with your own mortality changes your life overnight.

Bad things do happen to good people. This usually happens in a random and inexplicable way.

Why me?

The first noble truth of Buddhism is *to live is to suffer.*

Accept that life is tough and sit with the dark moments. Give yourself permission to cry, swear, be angry, break things, or do all of the above, repeatedly. You may want to sulk or, as I prefer to say, *have a big sook!*

Acknowledge that life will never be the same.

You may need to stay in this dark stage for a while.

Everyone's experience is individual. There are no rules.

Give yourself enough time to grieve for the dramatic change in your life.

All emotions are okay: being overwhelmed, furious, bitter, twisted, envious, devastated, resentful, and traumatised.

You may find yourself travelling in and out of the stages of grief. There are usually five stages. They can occur in any order, for varying lengths of time, and sometimes all in one day.

Cancer forces vulnerability upon you. You most likely have a distrust of your body now, and you have to relearn to trust it.

The key is to find acceptance of your situation and be strengthened by this.

Easier said than done!

I write now in hindsight after being through cancer. I used old skills and found new ways to counteract the grief, the uncertainty, and the fear. I was offered and accepted a lot of help. I learnt to move on with greater gratitude and purpose. This was not easy, but it has changed me for the better.

I have also drawn upon insights from others who continue to live well with cancer. I hope that some of these strategies may improve your well-being along the way.

CHAPTER

2 CHOOSE NOT TO LET YOUR ILLNESS DEFINE YOU

> Only through experience of trial and suffering can the soul be strengthened, vision cleared, ambition inspired and success achieved.
>
> —Helen Keller

Woe is me.

It is completely normal to be sad when you have cancer. Sadness turns to depression when people don't feel they have a way forward. Up to 40 per cent of people with cancer become clinically depressed. Research shows that women with breast cancer whose depression improves live longer.

You can choose not to become a "victim" of your situation.

Stay involved in your everyday life activities as much as possible. You may have to say yes to fewer invitations, avoid large crowds, sit rather than stand, or leave social events early. As we are social creatures by nature, it is better to stay connected with people during difficult times.

Time magazine reported in 2016 that during illness social supports can help people manage with painful treatments and aid recovery from cancer.

You can actually choose the lens with which you perceive your illness. Some people choose to languish, and some people manage to flourish.

Think about what might replenish your body, mind, and soul.

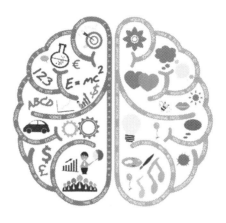

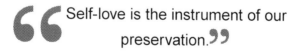
Self-love is the instrument of our preservation.

—Voltaire

Consider the importance of self-compassion. One of the world leaders in self-compassion, Kristin Nef, emphasizes the importance of treating yourself with as much kindness and care as you would show your best friend.

Don't give in to helplessness, and notice if you feel this way. Look for help to find positive directions ahead.

Avoid focussing on why things are so terrible for you.

You are not your disease, so don't let it define you.

Even on the worst day imaginable, you have a choice on how you approach it.

Plan in some guilty pleasures to balance out the bad times.

Lahna Catalino at the University of California has studied the pursuit of happiness. She found that positivity prioritisers, or those people who savour positive situations, have greater resources and experience more positive emotions.

Reflect on how people might feel when you walk into a room. They may feel uplifted, inspired, and interested. They may feel sorry for you if you continually complain and feel helpless. No one wants to be around a "misery guts." People will follow your lead if you respond in a more positive manner. Their response will follow suit from your mood.

Perhaps consider that the cancer experience may be an opportunity to become a better person.

> " When we are no longer able to change a situation—we are challenged to change ourselves. "
>
> —Viktor Frankl

CHAPTER 3

MAKE YOUR CANCER A PROJECT

> What is true for one may not be true for another, and a gift exists for each of us in discovering who we are, uniquely, as we find our way back into life.
>
> —Maria Sirois

Think of your illness as a time-limited project rather than a journey with a disease.

The treatment phase may be a twelve-month secondment from your usual life. Something like a gap year or a new job.

It may also be an ongoing project in which you have to customise your life to suit.

If you enjoy exercising, you could consider cancer to be a physical challenge like climbing a mountain or going on a trek. Your body is doing the equivalent of running a marathon, so perhaps imagine the treatment phase as a long-term sporting event.

Don't give in and be a passive recipient of treatment. Having a strong fighting spirit has been shown to translate to better outcomes during cancer.

Adopting an active approach to dealing with any stressful situation helps us cope better.

Having a sense of control will strengthen your well-being.

People develop grit and resilience rather than inherit it. This is a practised quality.

Belief plus effort and perseverance helps with recovery.

A New Frontier

We now know that we are not stuck with the genes we are born with. Epigenetics, meaning "control above the genes," is the study of how genes can be regulated. We are learning more about how genes can be switched on and off again.

Meditation has already been shown to switch off disease-causing genes.

Epigenetics will be a source of future discovery that may help address many medical mysteries and lead to further cures for cancer and other diseases.

There are stories of spectacular recoveries.

Imagine being one of them.

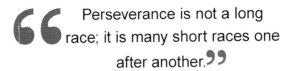

Perseverance is not a long race; it is many short races one after another.

—Walter Elliot

CHAPTER

4 DE-STRESS YOUR LIFE

No one saves us but ourselves.

—Buddha

Cancer induces a long-term stress reaction where the body continually activates the fight-or-flight response. This response is designed to deal with short-term stressors on the body. Chronic stress further suppresses the immune system. If there's ever a time you need your immune system to help you, it's when you have been diagnosed with cancer.

Reducing stress has to be an important goal.

Take regular time out to rest or spend time away from the demands of life.

Tips to Become More Resilient

- Give yourself permission to put yourself first.
- Outsource what you can to people who offer.
- Don't sweat the small stuff. Think about what is important to you right now.
- Aim to control the things you can control and let go of things you can't control.
- Is yes your automatic default position?
  Think twice before you say *yes* to people. Say *no* more readily.
- Settle for things not being perfect. Lower your expectations bar.
- Healthy, happy successful people simplify their lives.

- Avoid watching the news. It can have a toxic effect. If you really need news, just read headlines rather than details.
- Avoid freestyle Googling of cancer topics. This can be very unsettling and is rarely uplifting.

Massage

I recommend having as many massages as possible. Massage is most often not to be avoided during cancer. It is very beneficial. Don't let a massage therapist tell you that massage will spread the cancer. Get the go-ahead from your doctor before booking. This will mean you have a ready-made answer if a day spa suggests it can't treat you.

Touch releases oxytocin, sometimes known as the hormone of peace and trust. Oxytocin also counteracts the effect of the stress hormone cortisol.

If you're not up to a full conventional massage or can't lie on your stomach, find any part of your body that can be massaged, even if it's only your feet.

You may find bare scalp massage to be one of the most wonderful restorative experiences ever. I did, and it was seriously the *only* good thing about losing my hair!

After chemotherapy, you will never have to listen to a friend complain about a "bad hair" day ever again.

5 HARNESS YOUR PEOPLE POWER

Friendship doubles joy and cuts grief in half.

—Francis Bacon

The best predictor of well-being and happiness is the time you spend with other people in positive relationships.

Rally your troops.

Visitors are good for you.

Choose your people wisely.

Focus on positive-energy people.

Avoid the impact of negative nellies.

Set the conversation yourself. Friends and loved ones will be interested in your experience and keen to talk if you are. Most people won't ask you directly about your cancer. They will follow your lead.

> **"** Many of us are willing to extend a helping hand, but we're very reluctant to reach out for help when we need it ourselves. It's as if we've divided the world into "those who offer help" and "those who need help." The truth is that we are both.**"**

—Brené Brown, *The Gifts of Imperfection: Let Go of Who You Think You're Supposed to Be and Embrace Who You Are*

Consider carefully if you have the desire to cocoon yourself away from the world and avoid your support people. Sometimes the tendency is to "go to ground." This is totally understandable, but it is best to find a balance. The evidence is overwhelming that connection with loved ones and good friends is strengthening and supportive for those experiencing cancer.

Chances are you won't feel like contacting people, but maybe put the word out through a central friend or inner circle that you are happy for others to contact you.

Accept offers of meals readily. Not only do you benefit from the practical support but also from the huge dose of goodwill that comes with it. If someone offers to coordinate a food roster say, "Yes, please."

If you're not up to seeing people that day, leave a cooler or drop box at the front door with a note. People *will* understand.

Feel the love, and accept support.

Text or email people if it's easier. Lots of phone calls can be overwhelming and tiring.

Let people help if they offer. It's so much harder to do it alone. People want to help you in some way. It's their way of showing that they care. Some people show their love by doing things.

Phone uplifting or funny friends when you need a boost. Avoid your doom-and-gloom friends and family if you are not in the right frame of mind to deal with them.

Combine a catch-up with a friend with a nature walk.

If you enjoy social media, consider making a secret Facebook group to update family and friends. You'll be surprised how much support and encouragement this brings.

Make frequent lunch dates or coffee catch-ups happen.

Consider joining a cancer support group. They do not suit everyone. Notice how you feel afterwards. Hopefully you are energised or uplifted. If not maybe it's not for you.

A hug lasting more than twenty seconds will release oxytocin into your body and give you a feel-good boost.

❝I get by with a little help from
my friends.**❞**

—The Beatles

6 LINK WITH YOUR LOVED ONES

In time of test, family is best.

—Burmese proverb

Your family, and especially your partner, are going through a major challenge with you during your life-threatening illness. This can be the case even more so when the affected member of the family is the primary carer. Roles within families will change and routine is usually disrupted.

Carers also have an increased risk of developing anxiety and depression. So much focus is put on the person with the cancer that the needs of a partner may sometimes be overlooked. Studies have shown that spouses of breast cancer patients experienced as much distress as their wives. Spouses of colon cancer patients experienced even more distress.

Loved ones need to consider their own well-being and actively draw upon their supports. This might include a trusted friend or two to check in with how they are faring.

Try not to attend important medical appointments on your own. Important information may be forgotten or misunderstood. Take a partner or friend to take notes and to debrief with afterwards.

Remember that accepting practical help from your friends to deal with daily demands can also be of great benefit to your partner or family.

Relationships have a greater likelihood of being negatively challenged as a result of cancer.

Relationships can also be improved by deeper sharing of fears, hopes, and dreams. The major determinant of happiness over the lifespan has been proven to be the quality of people's close relationships.

If at all possible, keep children's routines as similar to normal as possible. Children will benefit from age-appropriate explanations of what you are going through.

Honesty is the best policy for children, but they can be spared unnecessary details. Kids are often more resilient than we imagine.

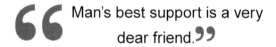 Man's best support is a very dear friend.

—Cicero

CHAPTER

7 TAKE CONTROL OF YOUR THOUGHTS

> Everything can be taken from a man but one thing: the last of the human freedoms—to choose one's attitude in any given set of circumstances, to choose one's own way.
>
> —Victor Frankl, *Man's Search for Meaning*

Your thoughts are transient. They come and go. It is normal for intrusive thoughts and images to predominate when you are diagnosed with cancer.

You have the choice to recognise and regulate your thoughts. You don't even have to believe your thoughts.

The major impact from your thoughts comes from your subconscious. This is said to dominate up to 95 per cent of the time. It is predicted that an individual has at least 60,000 thoughts per day. This translates to a lot of potential negative energy in your body if you don't tap into your inner thoughts.

Notice your inner voice or your subconscious thoughts.

What is its tone?
Is it sad?
Is it worried?
Is it anxious?

What message is it giving you?

Don't believe everything you think.

Perhaps ask your doctors what they think you should reasonably worry about, such as aches, pains, or other symptoms.

Avoid thinking traps.

- Recognise the futility of *what-if* thoughts. Notice if you are prone to doing this, and redirect your attention.
- Try visualizing positive outcomes instead.
- Do not assume that the worst-case scenario will be your outcome. People may do this in an attempt to protect themselves from disappointment if the worst-case scenario does come true. There may be very low likelihood that this will be the case, and this approach adds a lot of needless anxiety to a situation.

Look to shift your inner attention to something you appreciate or that restores you.

Set aside a time each day to remember a past time in your life when you were at your happiest.

> *You are always stronger and braver than*
> *you think you are.*

Cancer treatment often interferes with your thinking and memory capacity. This is a common side effect of chemotherapy and radiotherapy. This can be very frustrating. You may find yourself not being able to remember names and numbers. This is most commonly a temporary problem that improves slowly over time.

You can retrain your mind as if it is a muscle.

Think of having cancer as a "dose of cancer" or a "bout of cancer," an experience that is short term or time-limited and potentially recoverable.

Beware of the insidious detrimental effects of *nocebo* effect. Nocebo, or the dark side of placebo, means literally in Latin, "I shall cause harm."

Sometimes known as "medical hexing" or "pointing the bone," nocebo effect may bring the power of harmful belief into play.

Nocebo may be the delivery of negative news of side effects or prognoses that may actually worsen your condition. It may be a self-induced negative belief, such as "My disease is incurable" or "I am going to die."

One of the most important things for people with cancer is that the people around them have hope. Even if it is not hope for a long-term future, it is important to have hope for the most positive navigation through their illness as possible.

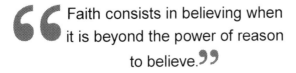

Faith consists in believing when it is beyond the power of reason to believe.

—Voltaire

CHAPTER

9 LEARN THE ACTION OF DISTRACTION

Be the change you want to see in the world.

—Gandhi

Excessive worry and rumination can keep you trapped in a negative state.

Take inspiration from Viktor Frankl, who was imprisoned in concentration camps for three years: force your thoughts to move to other subjects.

Learn to notice destructive thinking patterns.

Turn your attention to that which gives you joy.

Have a thinking project for when you wake up in the middle of the night to redirect your thoughts, such as the following:

- thinking of what you were grateful for that day, however small,
- thinking of an act of kindness for someone else that you may do the next day,
- thinking of what you can buy a friend or loved one for a birthday present, and
- planning your next birthday celebration.

> The word *mantra* comes from Sanskrit and literally means "mind instrument." Mantras can help us disconnect from constant streams of negative thought patterns cycling through our mind.

Adopt some mantras and use them as an antidote when bad thought cycle ruminations kick in.

- Aspire to inspire.
- Struggle is important for growth.
- This is an opportunity to be brave.
- Miracles do happen.
- Find peace in every breath.
- I am strong. I am invincible.
- Positive energy leads to positive life.

Have a slogan to visualise or recite.

When something bad happens, you have three choices. You can let it define you. You can let is destroy you. Or you can let it strengthen you.

The worst has happened, and I am still okay.

Have an uplifting song to sing to yourself to distract your thoughts.

You may have to dig deep to bring your best self forward. Tell yourself that giving in to misery is not an option.

Choose which emotions you want to bring to the forefront of your experience.

Focusing on humour in difficult situations is a great defence mechanism. Humour can increase your resilience. Smiling will actually make you feel better.

" Every time you are able to find some humour in a difficult situation, you win. **"**

—Unknown

10 ADOPT AN ATTITUDE OF GRATITUDE

A thankful heart is not only the greatest virtue, but the parent of all the other virtues.

—Cicero

Gratitude is the most studied and proven practice in positive psychology.

Sonja Lyubomirsky, author of *The How of Happiness*, has devoted her career to studying human happiness. Lyubomirsky has identified benefits of gratitude. It

- promotes savouring of positive life experiences,
- bolsters self-esteem,
- improves stress and trauma,
- encourages moral behaviour,
- helps strengthen social bonds,
- reduces social comparison, and
- diminishes negative emotions.

When dealing with cancer, there are a lot of *bad* experiences in your life.

Some experts say you may need up to five times more good to balance out the bad.

Start a gratitude journal. At night, write three things you were grateful for that day. Doing it just once or twice a week is enough to get significant benefit.

At the end of a day (or week), think of what went well.

Even if you cannot find anything to be grateful for, it is proven that it is the process of searching for things to be grateful for that has the positive impact for you.

Focus on your strengths and the tools that you have to help you get through the challenges ahead.

Keep in mind that it is not realistic to be "positive" all of the time. There are times of supercharged stress, such as new scans or doctors' appointments where your anxiety levels will understandably rise. The important thing is to develop your coping strategies to help manage fears at these strategic points.

Believe in the good, and try to be luckier.

Richard Wiseman, author of *The Luck Factor,* found that of the "unlucky" people who learned to behave like "lucky" people, 80 per cent were happier and more satisfied with their lives.

Tal Ben Shahar describes the characteristics of lucky people.

- They appreciate the meaning in coincidence.
- They vary their routines and are more mindful of the experience.
- They always look for the silver lining. Even if something bad happens to them, they consider that there could have been a worse outcome.

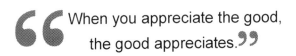

When you appreciate the good,
the good appreciates.

—Tal Ben Shahar

i AM
grateful

11 CULTIVATE YOUR COURAGE

Faith is a place of mystery, where we find the
courage to believe in what we cannot see and
the strength to let go of our fear of uncertainty.

—Brené Brown

Courage: (noun) The ability to do something that frightens one;
bravery. Strength in the face of pain or grief.

Some people seem to have courage available in large natural doses.
Others may have to dig deeper to be their bravest self. The good
news is that everyone has a large potential capacity for courage.
Like the cowardly lion in *The Wizard of Oz,* it's just a matter of
learning how to access your reservoir of courage from within.

Think of courage as a muscle. It's something you can exercise and
strengthen.

Having cancer can bolster your courage.

Remember a time in the past when you showed courage. Perhaps
write about this time.

Tell yourself repeatedly that you are brave and strong.

" We define ourselves by the best that is in us,
not the worst that has been done to us. **"**

—Edward Lewis

CHAPTER 12 TONE DOWN THE FEAR FACTOR

I learned that courage was not the absence of fear, but the triumph over it. The brave man is not he who does not feel afraid, but he who conquers that fear.

—Nelson Mandela

Negative thoughts and emotions are very normal when you have cancer. As a disease, cancer is more feared than other diseases. The idea is not to try to suppress these thoughts and attempt to be overly positive all of the time. Cancer has a dark and terrifying side. It is best to acknowledge your reactions and emotions and learn to let them occur. Notice them and let them sit and pass by without judgement.

It's good to acknowledge that your body has temporarily failed you. Over time, you learn to live with the background uncertainty that the cancer may return. The fear of this will often lessen over time. Learn to listen to your body and trust that it will try to cure you.

Fear stands for
False
Expectations
Appearing
Real

Avoid letting fear define your existence. Being consumed with fear will block your power to recover and heal. Notice when you are fearful and have ways to channel these emotions.

If you put a lot of energy into your experience being dreadful, then you are at risk of becoming a *catastrophiser.*

When the body is under stress, cortisol is released, which may cloud your thinking. This makes rational logical thinking difficult. If you work on being kinder to yourself, you will be more likely to let go of the fear.

Everyone will have a different comfort signature. Prayer works as a comfort for some people, but for others, it may be music, art, nature, or being immersed in science or technology.

" Fear keeps us focused on the past or worried about the future. "

—Thich Nhat Han

CHAPTER 13 REFRAME YOUR MINDSET

Take adversity and change it into opportunity.

—Winston Churchill

The Western approach to cancer is that it is an external disease attacking your body and must be fought like an enemy and destroyed. The Eastern approach looks at cancer more as an ally in the body's response to correct its physical and emotional imbalances from within.

It may help to reframe your thoughts on your illness with more of an integration of the Eastern framework.

Optimistic mindsets are associated with more positive healing responses and health outcomes. It takes effort and practice to change your mindset.

Dr. Lissa Rankin has widely studied the medical literature and asserts that it is possible to contribute to healing yourself. She asserts that "positive thinking does not equal false hope."

In the recovery period, it can be frustrating if you are told to *move on* or *put the cancer behind you*. This may take time and assistance, perhaps even counselling.

Tips for Shifting Your Mindset

- Challenge yourself to do something new.
- Notice whether your mindset is mainly optimistic or pessimistic.
- Recognise that you can choose how you perceive situations.
- Add the word *yet* to statements.

I am not good at exercising *yet*.

I am too busy to meditate *yet*.

It's not about aiming to be positive or happy all of the time. This is unrealistic. Accept that you will have *down days*. Have strategies that you can use during bad times.

Positivity Builders

- mindfulness
- looking for the silver lining
- surrounding yourself with optimistic people
- exercising
- feeling love, joy, and happiness
- getting outside into nature
- celebrating other people's success
- appreciating impermanence
- performing random acts of kindness

If you find yourself continually struggling with your anxiety and mindset, consider seeking professional counselling. There is no shame in doing this. It is a practical way to draw further on support people to speed up your emotional recovery.

"The same world, to different minds,
is a heaven, and a hell."

—Ralph Waldo Emerson

14 STAY IN THE MOMENT

> The secret of health for both mind and body
> is not to mourn for the past, worry about the
> future, or anticipate troubles, but to live in the
> present moment wisely and earnestly.
>
> —Buddha

Meditation optimises control of your attention. The aim is to turn your focus inward, concentrate on your breathing, and let go of the "white noise" in your head. Meditation is a general term that implies a practice that trains your mind to quieten your thoughts. Mindfulness, or being aware, allows you to be more conscious of your inner feelings and sensations rather than being controlled by your thoughts.

Brain MRIs have shown that meditation regulates the brain's flight-or-fight stress response.

Mindfulness meditation has been shown to strengthen your immune system.

A particular type of meditation called loving kindness (twenty minutes per day) has been shown by Barbara Frederickson to benefit people by

- improving relationships,
- increasing happiness and joy,
- decreasing depression and anxiety,

- enhancing a sense of purpose, and
- improving physical health.

When we breathe deeply, we induce the relaxation response (Benson 1975). The relaxation response counteracts the dramatic physiological responses to stress by slowing metabolic rate, reducing heart rate and blood pressure, and calming the body. Everyone has some capacity to reverse the impact of his or her stress.

Find what works to induce relaxation for you. Meditation is not for everyone. Other forms of relaxation can be used as well. Yoga is particularly effective as it combines inward focus, breathing, and stretching of the body.

> " Some of us think holding on makes us strong; but sometimes it is letting go."
>
> —Hermann Hesse

15 STRETCH AND MOVE YOUR BODY

> The best moments usually occur when a person's body or mind is stretched to its limits in a voluntary effort to accomplish something difficult and worthwhile. Optimal experience is thus something we make happen.
>
> —Mihaly Csikszentmihalyi

Our bodies are designed to be active. Keeping fit is probably the most important health intervention. Exercise is vital—before, during, and after cancer. The benefits are proven.

Exercise helps people recover faster and survive longer.

Exercise strengthens your immune system.

The endorphin release from exercise will make you feel better.

Exercise will reduce your stress hormones.

Exercise will reduce your tiredness and perhaps your nausea and other side effects from chemotherapy.

Exercise boosts the energy available to us.

Exercise will help you to sleep more soundly.

Exercise is one of the best ways to build self-esteem.

It is usually good to *push* yourself physically, but it is best to double-check with your doctor how hard you can exercise. He or she may give you a heart rate target or discuss the best type of exercise for you, such as cardio versus resistance.

Have a reason to get out of bed in the morning.

Arrange morning walks with friends.

Borrow a dog to walk if you don't have one.

Consider seeing an exercise physiologist or a personal trainer with specific health training.

Get a personal activity tracker, and preferably one that monitors heart rate.

Set some goals for movement each day. Document what you have achieved.

It is reported that alternative forms of exercise, such as yoga, tai chi, and Pilates, may provide even greater benefit than walking or running.

Physical exercise three times a week has the same effect as our most powerful psychiatric medications for depression.

If you are feeling tired, this is a reason *to* exercise and not an excuse *not to* exercise.

> **All truly great thoughts are conceived while walking.**
>
> —Nietzsche

CHAPTER 16

SLEEP TIGHT

Sleep is the best meditation.

—Dalai Lama

Sleep is the most restorative, but perhaps one of most elusive, pursuits when you have cancer. The nights can be long, and thoughts can get way out of control. The ruminations and the fear may intensify at night when it's much harder to distract yourself.

Lack of sleep affects mood, memory, and immune function. It is proven that your immunity is enhanced if you get more than seven hours sleep a night. For the majority of people, with fewer than six hours sleep, you're four times more likely to get a virus.

When you have cancer, you want to maximise your immunity as much as possible. Trying to find a way to sleep is an absolute priority.

Avoid screens for at least an hour before bed each night. Blue light, especially from screens, is the most disruptive. Think about not sleeping with your smartphone. Checking your phone and looking at a backlit phone before going to sleep has been proven to reduce your melatonin production by 38 per cent.

If you can't sleep, get out of bed and do something until the next wave of sleepiness arrives.

Consider using sleeping tablets for the acute stage. Perhaps try herbal supplements to start. Have half a sleeping tablet by your bed to take should you wake at 3 or 4 a.m. It's the early waking times that are exhausting. That's the time your body should be in the most restorative phase.

Tips for Better Sleep

- sleep apps
- meditation
- deep-breathing exercises
- self-hypnosis
- having a playlist of music to sleep to
- having a thought-distraction project

> When I'm worried and cannot sleep, I count my blessings instead of sheep.

—Bing Crosby

CHAPTER

17 SET GOALS FOR THE FUTURE

The best way to predict the future is to create it.

—Abraham Lincoln

Finishing treatment is often unexpectedly a very difficult stage. People think you should be celebrating when your treatment has finished, but it can be a hollow anticlimax.

Your dependence on active medical treatment, although demanding and traumatic, provides some reassurance that everything is being done to keep you alive. You may feel physically and mentally battered. Your focus has been on just getting through. Intensive medical support has been a constant for you. It can be hard to comprehend the next stage of your life.

Following medical treatment, it is important to continue an active coping approach. This means allowing for some natural doubt and anxieties but focusing on things you can do to improve your situation.

Research shows that people who pursue goals

- are happier,
- have greater well-being,
- are more resilient, and
- are more "future oriented."

Resilience is the ability to adapt well in the face of adversity.

Goals are related to things that you *want* to do rather than things that you feel you have to do.

A goal is just a dream without a plan.

Having a goal matters more than reaching a goal.

It is normal to feel challenged or even frightened to plan ahead.

Write down some goals for the future.

Plan some celebrations along the way. It could be "happy to be alive" days, birthdays, or anniversaries.

Do something that you have always been meaning to do.

Take up a new hobby.

Start a new positive habit, such as yoga, journaling, or a walking group.

Book a holiday (preferably somewhere warm and relaxing).

Sign up for a short course. There are free online courses in positive psychology. (An added bonus of getting your brain back into gear.)

" We're all co-creating this world and our lives within it through our emotions thoughts and actions. "

—Anita Moorjani

CHAPTER 18 WORK TOWARDS POST-TRAUMATIC GROWTH

Never let a good crisis go to waste.

—Anne Harbison

In Buddhism, hardship is compared metaphorically with being given a tool for growth.

A life-changing experience can lead to

- increased acceptance and openness,
- deeper emotional connection to oneself and others, and
- increased spirituality.

In a study of breast cancer survivors, those who found positive meaning in their illness showed better psychological and physical outcomes.

Reflect on the meaning of your experience.

Appeal to your higher purpose.

Many studies have been carried out on people's responses to adversity. There is a subgroup of people who not only recover but also are transformed in a more favourable way. These people seem to make the most of their misfortune. They take it as an opportunity to take their functioning to a higher level than before the hard times. Irish psychologist Maureen Gaffney calls this "flourishing under fire." Suffering and adversity may contribute to an individual's ability to flourish rather than preventing it.

Gaffney describes the five dimensions of post-traumatic growth:

- a deeper appreciation of life and changed priorities
- stronger, more intimate relationships with others
- a greater sense of your own personal strengths
- recognizing new possibilities and paths in your life
- development of wisdom

Hope springs eternal: (proverb) It is human nature to always to find fresh cause for optimism.

> "Life is never made unbearable by circumstances, but only by lack of meaning and purpose."
>
> —Viktor Frankl

CHAPTER 19 IDENTIFY YOUR IKIGAI

Follow your bliss, find where it is, and don't be afraid to follow it.

—Joseph Campbell

The Japanese concept of *ikigai* is simply defined as "a reason for being." It is believed that everyone has an ikigai, or a reason to get up in the morning. In Western terms, ikigai is more aligned with the notion of subjective well-being, with the addition of joy, meaning, and purpose in life. Ikigai can still be experienced during difficult times if one is moving forward with purpose and feeling that life is worthwhile.

Individuals who believe that their life is worth living tend to live longer.

What has been proven to contribute to happiness?

- deep authentic relationships
- self-compassion
- giving to others
- living in the moment
- meaningful experiences
- enjoyable activities
- a sense of achievement

The notion of Ikigai is represented visually by interconnecting circles. The aim is to consider all areas of the circles in order to fulfil your potential.

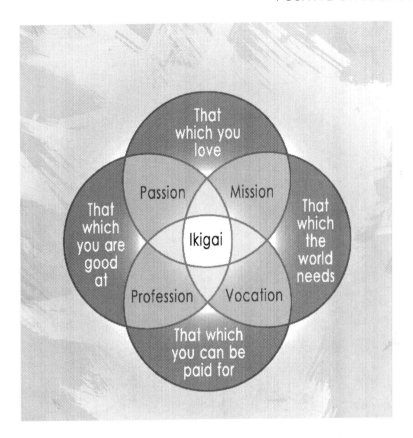

Toshimasa Sone coordinated a seven-year study of over 43,000 people in Japan and concluded that those people who believed their lives were worth living lived longer.

I believe that having the experience of cancer may fast-track a move towards finding your Ikigai.

It can be a time of deeper life reflection.

It may result in a forward momentum towards living your life more purposefully.

Raison d'etre means "reason to be."

CHAPTER

20 RETURN OF *THE BIG* C

Suffering does not negate what is good and rich in our world; what is good and rich in our world exists bounded by our suffering.

—Maria Sirois

A recurrence or progression of a cancer is devastating news. Nothing will soften the reality of this information. It will lead to a time of weighing up of treatment options, recalibration of hopes, and readjustment of plans for the future.

Being optimistic in your approach to cancer might seem inadequate at this time. My hope is that drawing upon positive psychology strategies may provide some extra tools to help when facing a dark stage of life.

Alastair Cunningham, of the Ontario Cancer Institute, discovered that patients who focussed on psychological interventions to bolster their response to cancer lived on average more than three times longer than was predicted.

This may be a point where it might be worth considering some professional counselling to assist with your adjustment to the next stage.

People do know more what to expect of treatment the second time around. There is, perhaps, less fear of the unknown. "I have been through this once, and I know I can do it again."

" If you're going through hell, keep going. "

—Winston Churchill

CHAPTER

21 AGAINST THE ODDS

> There are no incurable diseases, only incurable people.

> —Bernie Siegel, MD

Dr. Kelly Turner, from the University of California, spent over ten years of her life completing her PhD while studying people who defied the odds to recover from cancer. Of these seventy remarkable remissions, she identified seventy-five treatments from the extensive interviews with those individuals studied.

Six of these "treatments" were discovered to be "very frequent."

o changing diet
o deepening spirituality
o feeling love, joy, and happiness
o releasing repressed emotions
o taking herbs or supplements
o using intuition

Of particular note is the observation that out of these six treatments, four of them are emotional or spiritual and arguably quite achievable.

A message from this research is not to go out and pursue all of these treatments. This may lead to frustration and disappointment. It is important to find a way to approach your own situation that is doable and fits with your beliefs. Some of the modalities in this sample are controversial and may not fit with everyone's views. The uplifting message from this work is that there *are* people who might be considered "medical miracles." This is the message of hope.

66 I believe that tomorrow is another day and I believe in miracles. 99

—Audrey Hepburn

CHAPTER
22 TIPS FOR FRIENDS TO THE RESCUE

Cancer is a team sport.

—Dr. James Salwitz

Friends are seriously one of the best assets when you're going through cancer. The more connected you are with good friends, the more your resilience will be bolstered. Sometimes there can be a lot of people willing to help, but they may be unsure what to say or how to help. They may feel that visiting or phoning could be intrusive or demanding.

People with cancer often won't ask for help or say if they need assistance. They may have a fear of being a burden. They may not know what they need. It can just be another demand on their already depleted resources to try to think what you should do for them.

Lend a shoulder to cry on or an empathic ear to listen.

Send a text.

Send an email.

Send a second message even if you don't receive a response. When someone is in the throes of treatment, there is not much to write home about. They may receive a lot of messages. They may not feel up to responding, but they will appreciate the thoughtfulness of getting in touch. They might just be so busy that they haven't had a chance to reply to messages.

Write a card.

Send flowers or a pot plant.

Give a small gift.

It can be great if a close friend offers to be a central person to provide updates to a group of other friends. It can be very tiring relaying the same progress update many times over.

Check the level of information your friend would like passed on. Some people with cancer are very private; others are happy for details to be passed on.

Avoid making general offers or questions of how to help, such as "Let me know if you need anything" or "What can I do for you?"

For specific tips to support a friend with cancer, offer to do the following:

- start a food roster (more details below)
- drive children to school, sport, or activities
- vacuum the house
- do some gardening
- wash the dog
- do some ironing
- arrange a chemo date
- go to the supermarket for groceries or set up Internet grocery shopping on their computer
- take them for a walk
- take them to the gym

- go to a movie or bring one to the house
- set up a blog
- come and stay
- go for a drive
- have an overnight or weekend getaway

A food roster is some of the best help that you can receive.

Try to allow for variety. (There is only so much lasagne a family can eat.)

Be sensitive to changes in diet from the effects of chemotherapy. For example, people may want to eat less meat.

Check if there are family food allergies or dietary preferences.

Include written ingredients and preparation instructions.

Have a regular time for food to be delivered.

Consider leaving weekends off the roster. (There will be leftovers.)

Get ongoing feedback on likes and dislikes. Tastes may change along the way.

Use disposable containers where possible, as it can be demanding accumulating a collection of cookware.

Label returnable items with your name.

Set up a cooler and message board at the front door to signal when they aren't up to visitors.

Some people going through cancer are very sensitive to particular words or sentiments. This is a difficult issue for friends to predict. Some words might be an annoyance to one person but an inspiration to another.

Perhaps be wary of saying words like *survivor* or *battle*.

Some people don't like to be told that they are *brave* or *amazing*. Many people with cancer will find the word *journey* a cliché. In contrast, others will find this word gives a helpful description to their experience. Perhaps avoid the words *bucket list*.

Some people even struggle to say the word *cancer*, even if they have it. I did.

Be cautious of offering "helpful" advice about cures or treatments. Too much information can be overwhelming.

Have a discussion with your friend or loved one regarding if there are any words or phrases they dislike. They will readily tell you.

Most of all, don't overthink what *not* to say. Keep the communication channels open. Being an authentic, caring friend will outweigh any sensitivities that may arise.

" I floated twelve days without toothpaste or soap.
I practically almost had given up hope
When someone up high shouted, "Here!
Catch the rope!"
Then I knew that my troubles had
come to an end
And I climbed up the rope, calling,
"Thank you my friend! "

—Dr Seuss, *I Had Trouble in
Getting to Solla Sollew*

POSITIVE ONCOLOGY EXERCISES

Choose one exercise at a time. This is not a "one size fits all" section. Choose only the exercises that you like the sound of.

Find you own *formula*.

Best Moment Journal

Chances are your day may have been challenging and perhaps hideous in many ways, but no matter how bad, there is always a best moment to identify.

- This exercise gradually trains your mind to think more optimistically, induces positive emotions, and builds resilience

- You can describe your best moment in a few words or a few sentences, whatever you prefer.
- Start looking for your best moment early in the day. That way, you will be looking for even better moments as the day unfolds.

Funniest Moment List

Even on the darkest of days, funny things happen. You have to be attuned to look for them. Focus on the funny things that happen. No one else has to find them funny. Write them down. Black humour is therapeutic.

Norman Cousins famously overcame a life-threatening arthritic condition and pain by prescribing himself Marx Brothers films (and large doses of vitamin C).

Shortly after I was diagnosed with cancer, a friend suggested I could write a book about the funny things that happened along the way. From that day forward, my perspective changed. I was focused to look for funny moments.

Introduce Thirty Minutes of Humour into Each Day

Watch a funny sitcom.
Listen to comedy.
Talk to a funny friend.
Watch something funny on YouTube.

Introduce Pleasure Boosters into Your Treatment Routine

For every nasty procedure or treatment you undergo, reward yourself with an experience that brings you pleasure, with absolutely no guilt involved. You deserve it.

See a movie.
Buy a treat.
Have a massage.
Meet a special friend.

> **" Pleasure for man is not a luxury, but a profound psychological need. "**
>
> —Nathaniel Branden

Write Down One Thing You Are Looking Forward to Tomorrow

It is always possible to think of some things you are looking forward to the next day. It might be as simple as smelling your neighbour's roses, having a coffee at your favourite café, watching the sunset, burning your favourite candle, or watching your favourite comedy show or TED talk.

This exercise is proven to do the following:

o decrease pessimism,
o decrease negative effect over time, and
o decrease emotional exhaustion.

Dina Nir 2013

Write a Gratitude Letter

You will naturally feel grateful for the kindness people show you when you have cancer. It is probably not hard to think of dozens of people that you are grateful to.

Write one a letter thanking them for their support. Include examples of things they have done and perhaps the sad times and the funny times you have shared along the way.

Post it, email it, or consider visiting them to deliver the letter and read it out loud.

Journaling

The restorative power of journaling is well proven. It can help integrate your experience and process your emotions in a constructive way.

James Pennebaker demonstrated in 1997 that people who journaled for twenty minutes per day for four days were less anxious, were happier, had better relationships, and had stronger immune systems.

Buy a journal. Good stationery can be therapeutic. Write down how you feel. Don't overthink or censor it. Just write freely.

Deep Breathing/Meditation

Four deep abdominal breaths will induce relaxation and help reduce your fight-and-flight response.

Program more deep breathing into your day, including whilst waiting at red lights when driving, each time your computer starts up, at the supermarket checkout, and when you initially lie down in bed at night.

Hypnosis

Hypnosis is like a deep state of relaxation. It is the process of inducing an altered state of consciousness that promotes flexibility in shifting mindset, emotional reactions, and behaviours. Hypnosis has been used successfully during chemotherapy to reduce symptoms of nausea and fatigue and to enhance the body's healing powers.

David Spiegel, psychiatrist and researcher at Stanford University, followed eighty-six women with breast cancer for a period of ten years. Those who received group therapy and lessons in self-hypnosis lived an average of twice as long as those who were given only traditional medical treatment. Spiegel described himself as "stunned" at this finding, which contradicted his expectations.

Hypnosis CDs for cancer may be purchased commercially. Even better, try to find a clinically qualified hypnosis practitioner to write and record an individualised script for you. It can easily be recorded on your smartphone and used as a self-hypnosis script during your treatment. Hypnosis can also be very effective for pain relief and for sleep induction.

Guided Imagery Exercise

Visualise yourself in a favourite relaxing place. It may be lying on warm sand on a beautiful beach or relaxing in a rainforest with the beauty of nature around you. Whilst breathing deeply, imagine a soothing, healing, coloured gel is entering your body through the tips of your toes. As it makes it way through your feet and along your legs, it relaxes, soothes, and nourishes your tired body. You can feel the gel revitalising and healing each cell as it makes its way throughout your entire body—down your arms to the tips of your fingers and through all of your organs, muscles, and tissues. It may help to think of the gel washing over the white cells as your immune system army. As the gel warms and replenishes your "white knights," your body is strengthened. You are able to fight disease more effectively.

You may like to try this exercise in conjunction with progressive muscle relaxation.

Imagine yourself on top of a high mountain, sitting in the sunshine with a gentle breeze on your face. Take three deep breaths. Know that you have climbed this mountain. Slowly and steadily, with the support of loved ones around you, feel the pride of the achievement. Marvel at the wonder of the view. Notice how strong and resilient you feel.

Make up or find a script that works for you. Record it and listen to the visualisation with headphones while you are having chemo or when going to sleep at night.

Even better, get your partner or another loved one to read it out loud whilst you are having chemo.

Write a Self-Compassion Letter to Yourself

This exercise is particularly good if you are prone to negative self-talk. Imagine that you are your most supportive and empathic friend. This friend really understands you, has unlimited compassion for you, and knows all of your perceived inadequacies. Write a supportive letter to yourself whilst pretending you are this friend with a tone of unconditional acceptance and empathy.

Identify and Release Your Emotions

Identify and write down the emotions that you are feeling at defined points throughout your day. Acknowledging negative emotions and describing them will usually cause them to diminish in intensity. Notice how many positive emotions you are experiencing and work on other exercises to help increase your positive emotions.

Loving Kindness Strategies

Choose two people a day and wish for them to be healthy and happy. You just have to wish to yourself, not out loud.

Make Some Music Playlists

- o   songs to cry to
- o   songs to inspire me
- o   songs to energize me
- o   songs to relax me

Sing and Dance

Singing and dancing have physical and psychological benefits. Music is proven to be useful as a mood enhancer.

Sing in the shower.
Sing along in the car.
Sing in a choir. This has supercharged benefits.

Dance when you are in the house on your own.
Dance with your partner.
If you are not up to physical exertion, dance "on the inside."

Make a Positivity Portfolio

This may be a collection of favourite or uplifting songs, quotes, posters, artworks, candles, poems, letters, or objects.

Have a special place in your house where you keep your portfolio. Ensure there's a comfy spot to sit. Go there when you are feeling flat or need a lift. This could double as a meditation place.

Awe-Inspiring Exercises

Awe is an emotion related to feelings of fascination and wonder. The emotion of awe is known to have many positive benefits.

Think of an awe-inspiring time in your life and write about it for five minutes.

I remember a time when …

Watch awe-inspiring videos for half an hour a day. Google "awe-inspiring videos."

Have an awe-inspiring nature experience.

Walk or get driven to a favourite place, such as large trees in a forest or a panoramic view.

Set out to see as many sunrises and sunsets as possible.

Best Possible Self Exercise

Think about your life in the future. Imagine that everything has gone as well as it possibly could. You have worked hard and succeeded at accomplishing all of your life goals. Think of this as the realization of all of your life dreams.

Now write for twenty minutes about what you have imagined.

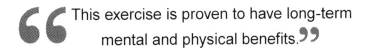 This exercise is proven to have long-term mental and physical benefits.

—Dr. Laura King

Reflect on Your Progress

Mark your calendar or set an alarm in your phone for six months away to evaluate the changes in your life. Aim to share your progress with a trusted friend or relative.

FURTHER READING

Cure: A Journey into the Science of Mind over Body, Jo Marchant

You Are the Placebo: Making Your Mind Matter, Dr. Joe Dispenza

You Can Heal Your Life, Louise Hay

Dying to Be Me: My Journey from Cancer to Near Death to True Healing, Anita Moorjani

Mind over Medicine: Scientific Proof You Can Heal Yourself, Lissa Rankin

Conquering Cancer: Developing Your Will to Live, Jeffrey Hodges and Lisa Briggs

Being Happy: You Don't Have to Be Perfect to Lead a Richer, Happier Life, Tal Ben Shahar

The How of Happiness, Sonja Lyubomirsky

A Short Course in Happiness after Loss: And Other Dark, Difficult Times, Maria Sirois

Writing to Heal: A Guided Journal for Recovering from Trauma and Emotional Upheaval, James Pennebaker

Man's Search for Meaning, Viktor Frankl

Mindset: The New Psychology of Success, Carol Dweck

Flourishing: How to Achieve a Deeper Sense of Well-being and Purpose—Even When Facing Adversity, Maureen Gaffney

Happier at Home, Gretchen Rubin

What Doesn't Kill Us: The New Psychology of Posttraumatic Growth, Stephen Joseph

The Whole Health Life Book: How You Can Learn to Get Healthy, Find Balance and Live Better in the Crazy, Busy, Modern World, Shannon Harvey

Supersurvivors: The Surprising Link between Suffering and Success, David Feldman and Lee Daniel Kravetz

The Motivation Manifesto: 9 Declarations to Claim Your Personal Power, Brendon Burchard

The MindBody Code: How to Change the Beliefs That Limit Your Health, Longevity, and Success, Dr. Mario Martinez

Tibetan Book of Living and Dying, Sogyal Rinpoche

Hardwiring Happiness, Rick Hanson

My Stroke of Insight, Jill Bolte Taylor

The Luck Factory, Richard Wiseman

The Genie in Your Genes: Epigenetic Medicine and the New Biology of Intention, Dawson Church

The Way of the Peaceful Warrior, Dan Millman

The Year of Magical Thinking, Joan Didion

FURTHER LISTENING

Meditations for Manic Motorists: In Car Relaxation Techniques, David Michie

Health Journeys' guided imagery audio series, Belleruth Naparstek

Radical Remission: Surviving Cancer against All Odds, Kelly Turner

FURTHER WATCHING

The Connection Documentary, Shannon Harvey

https://www.theconnection.tv

TED Talks on YouTube

How to Stay Calm When You Know You'll Be Stressed, Daniel Levitin, TED 2015

The Shocking Truth about Your Health, Lissa Rankin, TEDx 2011

Yes, I Survived Cancer. But That Doesn't Define Me, Debra Jarvis, TEDMED 2014

The Power of Vulnerability, Brené Brown, TEDx Houston 2010

How to Live to Be 100+, Dan Buettner, TED 2010

ABOUT THE AUTHOR

In *Positive Oncology: An Optimistic Approach to the Big C*, Sue Mackey draws on her personal experience to provide a succinct guide to increasing coping skills and emotional resilience during cancer. Sue is a practice manager, speaker, and former nurse educator. During her nursing career, she specialized in intensive care and coronary care. She and her husband, Chris, a clinical psychologist, run a large psychology clinic in Geelong, Australia.

Sue developed triple negative breast cancer in 2013. Her cancer treatment included five months of chemotherapy followed by mastectomy, radiotherapy, and further reconstructive surgery. She was able to draw upon her knowledge of positive psychology and her supports over this time. Sue set out to build upon these resources after cancer and completed a certificate in positive psychology through the Wholebeing Institute.

This book is written with optimism filled with strategies for developing the power of one's own resources in the face of a life-threatening illness.

Printed in the United States
By Bookmasters